Resilience Is An Elastic Experience

Devany Bright

BookLeaf Publishing

India | USA | UK

Made with ❤ on the BookLeaf Publishing Platform
www.bookleafpub.in
www.bookleafpub.com

Dedication

I dedicate this book to you.

Preface

Sometimes all we have is the past to help us move forward, and sometimes all we can do is hope for a better tomorrow. I believe that every day is an opportunity to reinvent yourself. There are graveyards full of people I used to be and I find an enormous amount of comfort in that.

I've come to learn we attract what we are, not what we want or need. After "blowing my life up," I found myself completely alone on a path of self discovery. I kept my head high, looked for signs, and remembered how LUCKY I am to be me.

This book is a series of poems I wrote that remind me who I am.

Acknowledgements

First and foremost, I would like to thank myself.

feelings pass in ninety seconds

so tell yourself a story that sticks

the choice is yours but so in the consequence

what doesn't kill you make you realize softness is a gift

If you would have said,
" This will be your life."
I wouldn't have believed you.

If you would have said,
" Everything collapses, protect your heart."
I might have believed you

When you said,
"You scared me."
I believed you.

Sometimes things fall apart.

Some seasons you get buried.

Some seasons you restart.

11:21 AM

Two hundred and seventy three

Finally today I felt free

The moon is full in leo

Divine timing loves me

Nines are theming

Resonating everywhere

The snake has shed

Something soft rests her head

Grace

3:23 AM

It starts in my chest
A feeling so sharp
It shocks my core

The sensation sinks to my hips
Calcifying memories down there
I sit in horror in the silence

It's dark until it's not
Spirit shows me hues
cry, shake, shift, release
I purge myself of you

3:45 AM

I never wrote a five year plan

I blinked and seven years passed

"Just get the degree."

I tried really

College isn't for me

I've learned experiencing something and having it be my reality is key

4:44 AM

It's okay to embarrass yourself
In the pursuit of human connection
love heals hatred and misery

The truth is hard to swallow
When you're choking on your pride
resilience is an elastic experience

You don't have to punish yourself
For not having the life you thought you'd have
don't identify with what limits you

You can move past any challenge and learn to love
Yourself the way you deserve to be loved
there is strength in walking away

Sometimes the moments that change everything
Are the ones you're most grateful for later
everything works out in my favor

8:14 AM

The raven crows

The sun shines

Blue lotus tea

Ganja, grounded, grateful.

Slow mornings love me

7:05 PM

Our choices put things in motion

Our thoughts spin the earth

Our actions open up different paths

Our emotions protect us during setback

Our past is of no consequence

7:20 PM

A crack in the foundation
leading several generations back

Doing the work
purifying our womb space

Alcehmizing the pain
shedding the hurt

My heart splits open.

8:45 AM

I didn't learn how to self love

My inner flame lacked control

I was the match that started the wildfires

Everyday is a new opportunity

I taught myself that darkness dies in the light

The cycle was always the same

Shame, hurt, humiliation.

Bottled up so deep

Writing transmutes every low frequency

4:46 PM

I find myself
in movement

The memories surface
downloads overwhelm

Procrastination isolation disassociation
awareness meditation

Mind body soul
flowing growing

Close past cycles
or suffer

9:01 PM

Recreate yourself

New you

New chapters

New levels of abundance

10:06 PM

The fire of your heart takes form in your hands

They touch those you love

Lift and position your pencil

Helping to articulate your thoughts and voice

Creating a sense of belonging

I know we're strangers now but
the sky remains bold and blue.

A forehead kiss from the morning sun and
poof.

Every vertebrae in my spine tingles
"Losing people is a form of protection too."

6:58 PM

Whatever you're seeking is already obsessed with you

If it's meant to be it will be

Regardless of setbacks

Anything meant for you will never pass you by

Stop pouring into cups that leave you empty

Embrace your mistakes to discover better paths

1:06 PM

Examine the rubble

Build on what's left

Don't take rejection personal

Close past cycles

Catapult forward with intent

5:48 AM

As slow as possible
As safe as possible
As soft as possible

Grow before you suffer

10:13 PM

Trust yourself

Love yourself

Forgive yourself

Only up from here

6:05 PM

It started with me broke and broken
At 25
Deciding between the backseat of my car or the motel 8

It led me to the city
A travel contract
Six weeks of isolation that flipped my script

It's only heavy because you
Are deciding over and over again
To carry it

I took my power back
A spiritual awakening
The pheonix that rose from the ashes

I hope you find peace
In the struggles
You never speak of

4:44 AM

It's okay to embarrass yourself
In the pursuit of human connection
    love heals hatred and misery

The truth is hard to swallow
When you're choking on your pride
    resilience is an elastic experience

You don't have to punish yourself
For not having the life you thought you'd have
    don't identify with what limits you

You can move past any challenge and learn to love
Yourself the way you deserve to be loved
    there is strength in walking away

Sometimes the moments that change everything
Are the ones you're most grateful for later
    everything works out in my favor

9 789369 545421